INTERNET BUSINESS SHORTCUTS

Make Decent Money Online Without Taking Years to Get There

I0464789

BY: BUCK FLOGGING

www.archangelink.com

www.buckbooks.net

Published by Archangel Ink
ISBN: 1503144208
ISBN-13: 978-1503144200

Table of Contents

4

Introduction

I first started out online by doing some blogging. Eww. Before blogging, life was good. I traveled the world, lived in nice places, did cool things that everyone envied, and otherwise lived the dream. I was poor, but turns out you really don't need that much money to hang out on a beach in Maui all day, hike around in some of the world's most remote and beautiful places for weeks at a time, or even ski every day once you've bought some decent equipment and found a way to weasel your way into ownership of a free season ski pass.

But that computer ruined it all.

The computer had me seeking to somehow better my life through a screen. I thought it would be cool to exercise my brain muscle for once and began researching stuff and writing my thoughts about it on a blog every week or so.

I blogged for months and months before I even realized that it was possible to make money with a blog. I found out about these Google adword things and put some on my blog. Within a year I hadn't even made the minimum to receive payment. I yanked the stupid, spammy ads down from the blog.

Then I found out about making money as an Amazon Associate. Cleverly, I threw a little widget in the sidebar of my blog labelled "Approved Products" or something like that, with several books that I liked and a bucket of coconut oil or something on display. For every thousand visits I got, I was making like $5. But before that sweet moolah would even come trickling in, Colorado, my state of residence at the time, and Amazon, just couldn't come to terms. My Amazon Associates account was cancelled, and I was no longer eligible to earn this hefty sum from my blog.

At the start of the third year, I created a fancy $99 annual paid membership to access my private monthly newsletter and wrote my first eBook—sold on my site as a pdf download for $19.99. I made about $1,000 on the eBook that first year and was really raking it in with the 30 newsletter subscribers I managed to hoodwink into signing up for the whole enchilada.

Yes ladies and gentlemen, I, Buck Flogging, big dick playa that I may be now, operated an online business for two years before I made three figures. The third year brought in four figures. The fourth year I made it to $23,000. In the fifth year I made $40,000. In the sixth year I brought in around $80,000 I think, and it wasn't until the seventh year that I made it all the way to six figures—but by then I had paid help and an affiliate program that ate up a large chunk of that burrito.

Sadly, after taking seven years to reach a pretty decent income with my online business, I was pretty damn sick of that online business. I wanted to do something new. So I did something new. Lots of somethings new. Did it take me another seven years to reach the point of making a decent income with these new ventures? No way!

My first online business—its structure, my branding, and just about everything about it—was really limiting. Yes, the growth rate was strong, and I could have kept it growing, and it could have paid my bills for a lifetime I'm certain. But it just didn't have that much potential to really do anything special, I was bored with it, it took a lot of upkeep, and, most importantly, with the wealth of observation and experience I had amassed on what does and does not work (for me and for others that I've followed for many years), I knew I could do much better. And I knew I could make my new endeavors much more successful in much less time.

I always used to say, when people asked me what I thought was key to my success, "Man, if I knew then what I know now I could have achieved everything that took me seven years to achieve in six months flat." And it's true. In fact, I started three things in 2014—one in January, one in March, and one at the end of May—and all three of them are doing better than my original business was after four years of hard work. The business I launched on May 30, with a website that took four hours to construct, already rivals the income I was seeing at the peak of my first business in year seven.

So I think it's time to share some of these "shortcuts" in a book. It might help you too become a lazy out-of-shape computer zombie that rarely goes outdoors and sleeps well beyond noon every day that no longer does any cool stuff, and with an investment of 99 cents and maybe an hour of your time if you read as slowly as I do, you can feel pretty privileged to learn lessons that took me from age 28 to 35 to get a handle on.

I make fun of myself, and make my life sound horribly worse than it was before I started pursuing the internet business dream, because I do think the "make money from home" craze is getting a little carried away. Yeah, it's cool. Yeah, I'm lucky. But it's not such a glamorous existence that it deserves glorification and worship. Just had to get that out of the way before we start. I'm not trying to create some kind of happily-ever-after hype machine. My life was a lot more like Richard Branson's when I got paid by the hour.

And you may be asking yourself, "Why the multiple references to Mexican food in the introduction Buck?"

And to that I can only reply, "I don't know. Fucking hungry I guess. It's not like you crave Japanese food when you're really hungry. If you noticed and were asking me that question, you're probably pretty fucking hungry, too. Grab a Snickers or something. Mmm. Snickers sounds good. I'd have to leave the house though. Screw that. It's the weekend. There could be people out there. No way man. I don't like it when they look at me. They're always looking at me!"

Okay, you don't have to be a creepy, reclusive weirdo that wears the same pair of unwashed shorts for weeks at a time like me if you earn some money from an internet-based business. Speaking of earning some money from an internet-based business, I better wrap up the burrito talk and get going before you stop reading. Hang in there. I've got some good stuff coming.

Scout Your Niche

Scouting your niche is the most amazing "hack" ever for expediting your success online. The biggest mistake I made when I started an online business—and mind you, I wasn't really intentionally starting an online business at the time, just sort of piddling with a little online journaling hobby more or less—I was on a one man island. I didn't know what existed beyond my personal blog. I didn't care. I was just doing my thing—doing my research, writing my posts, and waiting for the world to discover me.

I wrote at least 50 posts before the first person of influence found me. He thought what I was writing was pretty cool, and he just so happened to be the moderator of a pretty large Yahoo group. Do those even still exist?

Anyway, he told the group that I was writing some interesting stuff, took an interest in me, started commenting on my blog furiously, and we had some great discourse going that the guy's group really enjoyed. My traffic jumped from only about 30-100 visits per day to 300 overnight, and it stayed there.

Then I blogged at 300 visits per day until the next person of influence discovered me, or someone linked to an article of mine on another big site, or something similar.

Those events also increased the amount of traffic I got from search engines, magically. Basically, the only thing that ever got me any exposure was when someone else, who had worked for years to build up an audience, let people know about me.

But it wasn't until 2010 when I was ready to start making enough money to support myself with this hobby of mine, that I really had my back pressed up against the wall. My first year of really trying to make money, year three in my online adventures, was 2009. That was the year I made a measly four figures and was pretty down in the mouth about the success I had envisioned for myself before I began. And in 2010, my savings money down to the triple digits, desperation struck.

I had observed that comments on other sites linking back to mine had worked really well. I had noticed that just one person with an audience telling people about me had the power to increase my traffic on a permanent basis in a single day. With these observations, I decided to finally do what you should do before you ever even think about starting an online business of any kind—I identified the medium and large-sized influencers in my niche.

Back then I was using Blogger, and I followed about 100 blogs. You can actually see most of the blogs I decided to follow here: http://bit.ly/1EjbSAm.

I got to know all of the people in my niche. The ones I didn't agree with, I went and loudly disagreed in the comments on their blogs. Other bloggers that I liked I formed alliances with. I created a big stir, and soon there were people out there writing about me (both good and bad), inviting me to guest post on their blogs, and inviting me to be on their podcasts. I went from 300 visits per day on my site to over 1,000 per day. My revenue went from a few hundred per month to right around $2,000, which was just enough to meet my minimum survival salary.

So get this. In 38 months I only got to the point where I was making $300-400 per month, and in 30 days got it up to $2,000. I wasn't doing anything particularly miraculous either. I was just working hard to get my message out, be heard, and network with those in my niche that had a larger audience than my own. They had worked hard and done some smart things to gather an audience, and I was able to tap into years of their dedication with a single guest post, interview, and in some cases a particularly meaty comment or two. That's all it took.

Okay, so that's just with a blog and a message. Obviously not all online businesses revolve around selling a few eBooks or advertising.

Now I'm not exaggerating when I say this, because it's absolutely true. My business that I started in January with my partner Rob got beyond $2,000 per month with just two emails. Each took me around 5-10 minutes to write.

Shoat Cutz Bitches! (SCB)

Along the way, Rob (who was my first hired assistant back in 2012) and I had figured out how to make audiobooks, as well as turn eBooks into print-on-demand paperbacks. We decided that we should start a little business providing audiobook and paperback services among other publishing menu items that we had mastered in the year prior.

I was and still am completely sold on this business compared to my first, as we're dealing with high dollar value services that in turn help people make more money. That's an easy sell. People will always part ways with larger sums of money, and let go of it easier, when they know it will result in a profit just a few months down the road.

Plus, when dealing with clients that are going to spend hundreds and even thousands of dollars, paid advertising becomes much more viable, the work you put into getting "discovered" pays off big, and because we were offering a really good service that typically costs an arm and a leg, we were in a great position to do favors for the right influencers.

Our target market was indie authors—or self-published authors if you will. So what did I do? I halfassedly researched some of the key players in the indie author community. By key players, I mean people that had amassed an audience of indie authors that might be interested in, and could benefit from, our services. And then, I emailed them, offering one some unsolicited advice that can be shortened to "Your books aren't in paperback or audiobook and you're selling over 1,000 kindle copies per day. Dafuq you thinking bro?" and the other a favor— "Hey, let us turn one of your books into an audiobook and you can see how well it sells."

Favors are great, as they leave the other person thinking that you are awesome, and that you need to be repaid somehow. The unsolicited advice I offered to the other influencer in indie publishing was met with hesitation, but he did decide to use our services for the creation of one audiobook and one paperback. Of course it sold like crazy just as I said it would. I had added paperback and audiobook versions on ten of my own books, and knew from experience that adding a format will typically tack on 10% or more to what you're already making on Kindle per format. Since the first tester book was making $200 per day on Kindle, I wasn't the least bit concerned as to whether or not he'd get his money back.

Anyway, we ended up doing a bunch of his books in audiobook and paperback, and now he's making more than $5,000/month from adding the two formats.

So, you see, emailing these two people resulted in business going from zero to several thousand bucks per month in only a couple months. How? Both of the people I contacted, being pleased with the service we had provided, and being in communication with thousands of others that could benefit from our services, let them know about us. A strong endorsement from someone that has established great trust with a sizeable audience is worth its weight in gold. I'll take ten web hits backed by someone's trusted authority over 1,000 from random web surfers searching stuff on Google any day of the week.

This is what we've gotten from those two emails since they were sent out in January:

1. Over 50 audiobook projects (around $25,000)
2. Around ten paperback formatting jobs ($1,500)
3. Four podcast appearances
4. Two guest blog posting opportunities
5. Publicity at multiple writer conferences
6. Several thousand email subscribers for www.buckbooks.net (I make about 50 cents per month, per subscriber)
7. Publishing contracts on more than ten books

That's just a partial laundry list of things that have come from those two emails, and that's just what has come in since they were sent out in January. Our relationship with these two guys grows and strengthens every day. I consider them to be two of the closest online relationships I have with anyone.

What I created with these two guys was a pair of mutually beneficial relationships. That will be the topic of the next chapter, but before we get there, let me lay out some guidance on how best to scout out your niche.

Before starting just about any online endeavor, you should spend at least a month completely immersed in your chosen area of focus—getting to know exactly who's out there—and making an exhaustive list of who's who. I recommend doing the following:

1. Start a spreadsheet with five columns: Name, website, email, Facebook, Twitter (if you're a real overachiever you can add YouTube, determine if the person has a podcast, 2. Linked In profiles, and all kinds of other things you think might be relevant or useful)
3. Google websites in your niche and see what you find
4. When you arrive on a related site, look for blog network badges, blog rolls (a list of sites the person likes), and anything you can click on that will take you to a related site so you can keep the scavenger hunt going—often you won't ever have to return to Google to fill out your spreadsheet
5. Follow all of these people/websites on social media
6. Find as many Linked In and Facebook groups as possible relating to your niche, and join them
7. Scratch your crotch a lot—I don't know if this helps, but I do it a lot and you never know, that just may be my secret to success
8. If I'm on your spreadsheet, just send money

Then, once you've compiled this burly mountain of information, it's time to start planning your strategy for contacting some of these people.

If you're just starting out, make sure that you are being reasonable. I'm very comfortable contacting some pretty big fish because I have extensive experience, valuable skills and services to offer, and am just not intimidated by contacting others because of what I have achieved. You really can't fake confidence, you have to earn it.

In other words, don't rush out to contact Oprah. In fact, most of the people you contact will likely be people you've never heard of. That's actually a good thing. There is an endless abundance of medium-sized influencers on the internet. Medium-sized influencers are perfect because they are just relevant enough to spend time building a relationship with, but they aren't so big that they are untouchable. They actually will respond to personal emails and often take the time to exchange several messages with you. Good things will come of these exchanges if you have something that can be of benefit to them.

A decent medium-sized influencer might have 10,000 Likes on Facebook and a global Alexa ranking of 100,000-500,000. But you should also pay very careful attention to how many comments they get on their posts if applicable, and how many likes, comments, and shares they get on social media. These metrics show engagement, and engagement is more important than size. Hear me now, believe me later.

If you offer a medium-size influencer something of value, or you're just nice and cool and don't seem to be fishing for favors, you might find them willing to become an affiliate for your site, mention your posts or services on social media or on their blog, or invite you to post on their website or vice versa. This is how you get off to a good start in a short period of time. You can't just be a one person island waiting for the modern day Chris Columbus to stumble upon your work and tell the world. It can happen. It has happened. But it's not likely to happen to you unless what you're doing is truly special. What you're doing is probably not as special as you think it is!

Most importantly, be genuine. It's not like when I reached out to the aforementioned influencers in the indie publishing niche that I was thinking only of myself. I wasn't. My real persona beyond the façade of Buck Flogging the big dick gangsta is actually very sincere and generous, almost to a fault. And I can honestly say I love these guys. My girlfriend actually refers to one of them as my "boyfriend," as I really admire the guy and am always checking to see how his books are doing, reading his posts, and otherwise being a bit of a groupie.

So now you know who's who in your niche. That's a very important first step when you start any online business. Don't be lazy about this process. Be thorough. Put in the time. Grind it out until you're pretty sure your spreadsheet is an exhaustive compilation. And be on the lookout for new voices, faces, and entities to emerge.

If you have any extra time, are not in that big of a rush to work from your pajamas full time, and really want to do this up right, spend ample time actually reading and studying these sites, people, and entities. Watch their YouTube videos. Read a book of theirs. Really know who everyone on your spreadsheet is and what their message/service/angle is. Knowledge is power in this regard, as it will give you great ideas, give you a thorough education in and of itself, and will make your future attempts to network with these people easy breezy booby squeezie.

Before we continue, let's brainstorm a little bit about what kind of mutually beneficial relationship you could form with someone in your field.

Mutually Beneficial Relationships

Every internet entrepreneur essentially wants the same things: exposure, growth, subscribers, and followers. These things can collectively be called "leads," and leads are what later become sales if the person communicating with these leads is of high integrity, tasteful, shrewd, and offering something of value.

By offering audiobook and paperback production on eBooks already written, Rob and I had it easy. We were creating friggin' products for them to sell! We've taken it even further as of late by offering to create entire books from scratch for clients, published in three formats, and given a proper launch through Buck Books. Turnkey book production, basically.

So before you even bother to start contacting people in your niche in an attempt to network with them, you've got to be able to do something for them in return. If you can't, you might have some trouble making much headway with that spreadsheet you've constructed. But you could still invite yourself onto their podcasts or write some content for their sites for free—shortcuts we'll discuss in greater detail later on. If all else fails, write a post on your own site about how amazing "x" person or product is and contact the site owner to tell them about it. They'll probably feel compelled to show people on social media how awesome they are by directing them to your article. And something might come of it.

Okay, the only way I really know how to spew some ideas on how to create mutually beneficial relationships with people at the middle and top of your niche, and to get you on your way to building authentic relationships with influential people that can give your fledgling business some quick liftoff, is to do some scattered brainstorming using potential real life examples. These are all completely fictitious but realistic scenarios that you can hopefully learn from. Here goes:

Barb the editor

Barb is an editor. She's been doing it for years for a publishing company, but she's ready to start her own private gig as a freelancer. Her best bet is probably to identify the small publishers online or big authors in the niche she likes to edit for the best. Better yet, she might want to identify the top people that share author tips to a large community and offer to do some free editing for those people, hoping that, in return, those people will begin recommending her services if she does a great job for them.

Jenny the food blogger

Jenny can cook up a storm. She loves writing about food, sharing photos and recipes, and critiquing restaurant meals. She should probably scout out blog networks she can enter into to jumpstart her success. Or perhaps she can offer to write some free content for some popular foodie sites. She should definitely leave as many comments on other food blogs as is humanly possible. Another idea might be to host some kind of event or competition for the best food photos or recipes, inviting all of the big food bloggers to enter the competition and drive traffic over to vote for their favorites. This is a great way to get some big traffic, give each food blogger additional visibility to new food-loving audiences, and so on. She could even offer a big cash reward for the winners—worth it for all of the incoming links she'll get from foodie sites, jumpstarting her success.

Bob the healthy snacks guy

Bob has just created a line of healthy snacks featuring some miracle ingredient. I don't know. Maybe the dude is all about sneaking kale into stuff. Who knows what he's into? Bob should contact the big players in the healthy eating scene and send out samples of his products. He could create some kind of affiliate program, or perhaps just give away his stuff for super cheap on Amazon, organizing a big flash sale amongst the health food crowd—those people, in turn, making some Amazon Associates commission for promoting his products during the sale and getting them off to a good start.

I've had lots of samples and favors done for me, and I almost always reciprocate in some way. I've promoted everything from cookware to shoes from nice folks with original products that sent me some free goodies. Hey, when someone sends you handmade shoes that are custom built to a trace of your feet, you're gonna hook the dude up with a link in a blog post.

Dave the precious metals investor

Dave's an experienced precious metals investor, and is known for his great timing and ability to make forecasts in the market based on analyzing charts. Now he's wanting to share his valuable insights with subscribers willing to pay for his daily market forecasts. Maybe he could contact and get a huge precious metals dealer like Monex to promote his newsletter in exchange for promoting their services exclusively as his subscriber base grows. Or perhaps he could create an affiliate program where people in the precious metals investing community could get some of those subscriber fees by recommending his daily newsletter, and then get busy contacting as many people in that niche as possible.

Moonbeam the video blogger

Moonbeam is feeling fit and fabulous after four days on a vegan diet, and now she's ready to share her message of eternal youth with the masses on YouTube. She should contact some popular vegan zealots on YouTube and invite them to do a video interview while promoting their products and books for them. It's a great way for her to get seen by people that love to watch vegans talk about how awesome and spiritual it is to be a vegan. Better yet, maybe she could host some debates on her channel between various vegan vloggers, and stir up some controversy while getting thousands of views on the videos by people who rush over to see how the drama unfolds when starchy vegan goes up against fruity vegan, or whatever.

Dustin the ninja

Dustin is like an 8-degree blackbelt, having trained extensively at Roger Baker's Taekwondo and Pizza in Pensacola, FL. He has just created a 10-hour home training video that he would like to sell online. For Dustin, it makes the best sense to start networking with people in his niche and just letting them know about him. An affiliate program probably makes the most sense here, but there are a whole host of creative ideas that he could come up with. Perhaps he could even network with moderately popular martial arts vloggers and drive around the country filming a documentary that he could give away for free (that mentions his training course at the end, or requires a person to subscribe to an email list to view the free documentary—enabling him to later attempt to sell these leads his training course), with each vlogger sworn to tell their audiences about the free film when it debuts—increased visibility for everyone in the documentary.

Beth the essential oils member

Beth is thinking of signing up to become a Young Living essential oils wholesale member. For those of you that don't know, this is a network marketing scheme where you sign up distributors underneath you, and the more and better the distributors underneath you (in your "down line"), the more money you make. She's seen lots of her favorite bloggers kill it lately in the essential oils field. By far her best bet here is to find the right distributor to sign up under—as that person will then have a vested interest in her success, and so will several other big bloggers above her. She signs up and creates a free book about essential oils or perhaps an eCourse or video course. All of the bloggers above her promote the crap out of it. People flock to her eCourse, sign up for her newsletter, and in turn become both consumers and distributors themselves. Beth has nearly overnight success, and all of the bloggers that promoted her are making more money now, too.

Alicia the goat's milk beauty products maker

Alicia's daughter always broke out in a rash whenever she came in contact with some kind of commercial lotion or soap. So she started learning how to make her own, and lo and behold, her daughter uses them with no ill effects. Alicia is ready to start making these products commercially and selling them on Etsy, Amazon, eBay, her own website, or maybe all of the above. She should invest some time and at least $1,000 to send out free samples to as many relevant mommy, natural health, and crunchy granola bloggers she can. An affiliate program to go with that to help these bloggers earn some money from promoting her products should do the trick—if, of course, these are good products.

Sooooo, maybe these were some lousy examples, but hopefully you're seeing a pattern emerge. It's pretty simple really. Network with the right people, and make sure there's something in it for others to be helping your ass.

Most entrepreneurial endeavors online involve selling a product, a service, or rely upon selling advertising after gathering some good traffic. Selling a product is pretty easy if it's affordable to send out samples and create some kind of affiliate program for it to share profits with those helping you out. Selling a service is even easier, as you can do favors for the right people without sinking any money into it. Just your time.

And selling advertising of some sort, including being an affiliate for other people's products, is all about getting some traffic in. I'm talking about blogging, basically. This is the trickiest but probably the most common way to make money online, as you don't really have to be that great at anything (offer a service) or create some kind of nifty, original product. Still, most fellow bloggers in your niche know the deal, and will be quite friendly and easy to network with. They are always looking for content, more links to their sites, and more allies that are willing to share their content and drive traffic their way. Blog networks, which are dominating this realm these days, are something you may want to join right away—solving the whole "build mutually beneficial relationships with those in your niche" problem for you overnight. Your success is their success, and they'll go above and beyond to get you up and running in the shortest period of time possible.

The repeating theme, no matter what you do, is to reach out to people who already have established audiences that are interested in what you're writing about, educating people about, doing (as a service), or selling. Sure, you could probably be a loner and eventually reach the point of success, but why wait years when you can be well on your way in a matter of months?

Before we move on, I will share with you how my most profitable and innovative business works, which is www.buckbooks.net, kicking butt and taking names since May 30, 2014.

The Amazon Associates program pays 8.5% commission on everything bought by a customer who was referred to their site by you within 24 hours of clicking on one of your links. You don't have to tell everyone about some great expensive camera or new electronic device to make money. Just get them over there. A certain percentage will buy stuff, and you'll make some money.

My idea was to get a bunch of subscribers in, send them an email broadcast every day, and get as many of them as possible clicking on my links daily. Nothing is cheaper on Amazon than books, and in this case, these are urgent, 24-hour flash sales on books priced at 99 cents or less. I send out the email broadcast telling them to hurry and grab the book while it's on sale. I don't say too much about the books because I want them to click on my link to see what the book is—not see what the book is in the email itself and say, "Nope, not interested," before even clicking.

I make a little less than six cents per click typically, and get thousands of clicks per day. In the first full quarter I got over 350,000 clicks! In the first year of operation, Buck Books will easily exceed $100,000 in revenue, and the stage is set for making much more than that. Pretty cool since I've already cut my Buck Books workload down to just a few hours per week.

As you can see, to be successful, I need dem scriberz. To get dem scriberz, I need dat traffic sent to the site. So I have to be performing some kind of service to the people sending traffic to the site. You know, that whole mutually beneficial thing I've been preaching about.

That's easy. Authors need their books promoted to new eyes to get sales. Not only do I promote authors' books for free, but I also pay them $1 per subscriber that they refer to the site. They get not one, but two benefits for sending traffic over to Buck Books. I'm a helluva guy, it's true.

Anyway, only an idiot would give away much more than that about their own, profitable, not-particularly-hard-to-duplicate business that they just created. But I did want you to see that I network with authors and the people in their niches, provide a great, free service to them that results in not one but two forms of extra income, and all I ask in return is a little love so that I can keep the subscriber base growing and get more of those six-cent clicks. What's cool about it is that the bigger the subscriber base becomes, the better the service it is to authors. It should, in theory, get easier and easier as time goes on. What author would refuse to drive traffic over to Buck Books when I'm ready to feature their book to tens or even hundreds of thousands of highly-engaged subscribers, for FREE?!

Let's move on. Next are some of my tips for reaching out to people and actually getting a reply.

Making First Contact

"Hey dood,

I just downloaded your book. I could tell just from the description that it had to be pretty good stuff. I'm an author too and have just started branching out recently from my bread and butter (health and nutrition) and into writing about authorship, blogging, online entrepreneurship, etc. Just came out with a book called Kill Your Blog that you would probably appreciate.

Anyway, I'm going to read through your book when I get time. I have a feeling already that there will some kind of collaboration or mutually beneficial thing in store for us. I've been doing audiobooks lately for two big authorship authors that would probably be eager to promote your book, amongst other collaborations. I can tell that your book is an audiobook candidate right away

But I wanted to reach out and say hello. I'll let you know what I think of the book once I get through it."

That was a first email that I sent to Derek Murphy, author of Book Marketing is Dead and blogger at www.creativindie.com. I did end up narrating that book and producing it for free. I also connected him with some important people in his niche that he later met in person and built a good relationship with. I've since had him participate in an online event, he invited me to guest post on his blog, he put a quote of mine in one of his books, and he's recommended my audiobook services to other authors. That's just a short list of collaborations we've managed to put together, and we've got many more in store for the future I'm sure.

He of course replied, as I'm sure you've figured out by now.

So what is the secret to getting a reply with an unsolicited email to an influencer of some kind that could really help to shortcut success?

Firstly, I always write informally. It doesn't take much to instantly keep it from sounding like you are fishing for business or favors. By starting it, not just with dude, but with the intentionally-misspelled "dood," the tone for a casual conversation is set. That's a good thing. Being casual emanates confidence. And while getting an email with some kind of business proposition can sometimes be exciting, and it is possible to get a response, creating a simple human-to-human chat is much less likely to get ignored.

Think about it. Let's say you're hanging out in an elevator, and there is someone in the elevator you've never met. If he's wearing a suit and tie and turns around with a business card and some phony-sounding talk about a special opportunity he wants to talk to you about, your posture and body language is instantly going to become defensive and protective. That is going to be one uber uncomfortable elevator ride. Probably would have been less awkward if you had farted loud enough for him to hear and it really stunk, but neither of you said a word.

I assume that would be awkward, of course. I have no direct experience with such a thing. Everybody knows Buck Flogging's farts are completely odorless.

Nobody wants to be sold. Nobody wants to be treated like a customer. Nobody wants to be put into an awkward situation where they are pressured to do something that sounds bogus. The more obvious it is that someone is trying to sell something, the more repulsive it is. My worst experience was going into a sex toy shop with my girlfriend and being met with an aggressive sales pitch about the latest vibrators by a guy with the dental hygiene of a wild animal on meth. He could have been giving away $100 bills and I wouldn't have accepted one, thinking that it was some kind of trick—it was that aggressive, overtly commercial, and tasteless.

Don't be like that your first time reaching out to anyone! Or your second! And probably your third as well!

Secondly, you want to demonstrate confidence, and there is no better way to set the tone in a way that puts you on equal ground (even if you don't deserve to be) with the people you are reaching out to. The best way to demonstrate confidence is not to spout your accomplishments, but just be totally cool. I try to always start out conversations with something you would only say to an acquaintance that you feel comfortable around. That's different for everyone. It could be something clever. Something funny. While many may disagree, I think it's a terrible mistake to try to sound "professional." You're more likely to come off sounding like a wannabe at best, and a stiff business-ish swindler trying to pawn off a business card at worst.

Don't sell. Don't swindle. Your goal is to just make a new friend—a friend with similar interests and goals as your own. Your tone should be more like what you use amongst your Facebook friends. Be a little daring with your sense of humor. And hopefully you've oriented yourself to the person you are reaching out to contact, and you have a feel for their vibe and personality by having read a few articles and watched a few of their YouTube videos perhaps. Then you can meet them on their sense of humor, and ideally show that you are knowledgeable and appreciative of what it is they do or have said in the past.

I, for example, always make reference to 80's movies. People write to me all the time, but the ones that make a joke about an 80's movie or photoshop my head onto the body of a famous 80's movie character are much more memorable and likely to be friends of mine that I email to say hello to years down the road. Once I went on a road trip to meet some of my followers in person. One actually had a movie cued up, and he tested me to see if I knew what movie it was. Another was wearing a *Ghostbusters* shirt. It showed me that they knew me, liked me, got me, and appreciated not just what I had to say but who I was. It was flattery but at the same time it wasn't flattery, if you know what I mean. Those were real connections that I'll never forget. If any of those people called me up tomorrow I'd know immediately who they were and be ready to help them in any way I could. Make a real connection with a real human being. Whether it benefits you in some way or not doesn't matter. It's fun. Be fun. Be fun to communicate with. You'll form some strong bonds that will last a long time.

Thirdly, keep your first email or message to a new person you're reaching out to for the first time very brief. 100-200 words is probably a good range. It's enough to say something, but not so much that the person is compelled to skim or hit the back button altogether. People that are successful enough to matter but not so successful as to have someone filtering all of their emails for them, are typically busy people. Keep that in mind. It will save your time and theirs to keep communications brief. You're not trying to perform any magic on the first email anyway.

Your goal should simply be to get a reply. If you get a reply, the conversation has officially started. People are a lot more likely to ignore someone they've never communicated with than they are someone they have communicated with. Get them to communicate with you and you're on your way to establishing one of those glorious mutually beneficial relationships.

Speaking of getting a reply, that's what each of these tips are geared towards helping you achieve. Keep it short. Be fun and cool and someone that sounds interesting to communicate with. Be confident. No sales pitches. Did I mention that yet?

Lastly, and I hate to say "lastly" because I could probably go on for hours about subtle psychological aspects of communicating with others (it's more about YOU and your mindset than anything else), remember Buck Flogging's one rule that trumps them all when it comes to any online affairs: Quality trumps quantity every time.

Like I said before, I primarily built a recent business with two emails. I didn't need to contact everyone on my spreadsheet (although I wish I spent time contacting a lot more), and if I had tried to drop a copied and pasted "Hey there, how's it hangin'?" into 200 emails, I probably wouldn't have been successful with a single one. I wouldn't have stood out or gotten the amount of attention needed to really get somewhere with that person.

I honestly think it would be better to put your heart and soul into contacting one person than it would be to halfheartedly contact a thousand. Along the same lines, it's better to reach one reader or customer with something of memorable quality and distinction than it would be to get a thousand empty "hits" (they really should be called misses!) from a shallow ad campaign or super ninja SEO hacks or other garbage.

I believe the currency of the future when it comes to internet business will be honesty, integrity, and trustworthiness. Another word that comes to mind is "genuine." Entities that do not have such qualities will perish. Those that do are bound to find success. It may not be the fastest way to start rolling in the dough, but if you bring those qualities into heartfelt exchanges with individuals in your niche that you really, genuinely desire to provide some kind of assistance to, then you'll still get to a place of financial comfort in a hurry. More importantly, you and what you do will last—riding on the coattails of trust and loyalty.

Now go make some contact!

Next, let's talk about some specific things you can do that may give you a huge head start in a new internet venture.

Join a Network

Not that I would recommend becoming a blogger specifically. I am, as sure as my name is Buck Flogging, an eternal loather of blogging. But in the new world of blogging, it's all about being in a network. Whether you have products or services to sell or not, joining a blog network can be a great way to immediately waltz into a group of dedicated and influential allies.

Blog networks are basically an organized group of bloggers that work hard to cross-promote one another's sites, posts, and products. Usually the network will be themed somehow—such as a network of health bloggers, food bloggers, style bloggers, etc. A particularly huge blog network would be something like www.blogher.com, a network of bloggers who blog about all things woman.

Blog networks can be kind of annoying, stifling, and corporate-feeling. That sort of defies the idea of becoming a blogger in the first place. You might consider simply trying to network and form alliances with lone bloggers that aren't in a network. One way or another, blog network or not, you should be forming good, strong, mutually-beneficial relationships. I know literally hundreds of bloggers making more than $100,000 per year, and only a handful actually possess any real talent for it. They just teamed up with the right group of folks, got big in a hurry, and now the world is their oyster. They can take pretty much anything and turn it into profit at this point.

Basically, one of them will create some kind of product or event, and the other 50+ bloggers with over a million site hits per year, big subscriber lists, and huge followings on social media, team up to promote it. Everyone makes money. Everything they create is an instant success. Books, book bundles, Amazon products, online classes, summits, and even network marketing schemes are just a small sampling of how they make money off of the huge audiences they have amassed. It's pretty cool. It's without a doubt a great shortcut for the right type of online business.

Write a Kindle Book

Writing a short book and publishing it on Kindle can be a great way to jumpstart any online business. While everyone thinks that money is made from the sale of the book itself, there are many things that can be done to make more money *off* of the downloads of your book, than *from* the sales of your book directly.

Consider one client of mine. He has a video training course for sale on his website for $149. He also coaches people one-on-one for nearly $1,000. When we started working together he had virtually no following other than a few hundred people that had stumbled across him on Facebook and thought he had some cool things to say regarding his area of expertise.

Then we launched his book, which got thousands of 99-cent downloads during a total of two promotions in its first month out. His book still sells quite well, and since the launching of his book he's made $2-3 in website sales for every $1 in book sales. His book is usually priced pretty cheap so he'll get extra downloads, because the book sales alone are not the primary source of revenue generated by the book.

As you might guess, the same is true for Buck Flogging. Book sales are secondary to the thousands of dollars of business that these books of mine have generated. Amazon gives authors the ability to run free promotions on books for five days out of every ninety, which I have and will continue to take advantage of. This is the fourth book I've written, and all four of them will probably combine for more than 20,000 downloads in their first year—and that's a very small number as far as Kindle downloads go. With more effort, I could have taken this much farther. Under my real name I've had 5-day book promos that have been downloaded up to 20,000 times! In the future I hope to run free promos with twice that many downloads.

So let's say you have a product or service. Taking this idea a step further, it's also possible with a few simple steps and some patience, to get Amazon to permanently price your book at $0. Normally this isn't possible, as Amazon sets its minimum allowable price on eBooks at 99 cents. But via the exploitation of Amazon's dedication to price-matching, it's possible to submit your eBook to other sites, like Lulu, for free—and then report this price to Amazon. Well, you alone probably won't be enough to get them to price match, but if you can get a few dozen people to report the lower price elsewhere, it will likely take effect in a month or two after release.

With some promotion (Hey, I can help you there!), you can get that thing thousands of downloads after the price has dropped to zero, and hopefully it will continue to get downloaded thousands, or at the very least hundreds of times per day in perpetuity. I feel pretty confident that I could get a short, "permafree" Kindle book read by more people than any blog post. If it's a lead generator for high dollar products and services back on your website, this could be a very quick way to start earning some decent income online.

If I ever write a book that is really REALLY generating some revenue on an external website, rest assured I will stop selling the book immediately and give it away for free!

While this isn't a foolproof strategy, and a lot of things have to fall into place for this to really be firing on all cylinders, I do think many people underestimate how easily and quickly you can reach large volumes of potential customers with a Kindle book. Having a successful, well-reviewed book can also be a fantastic overall image enhancer. For those starting at ground zero and hoping to find a way to escape the rat race in favor of computer enslavement, it's certainly something I would consider.

Focus on Lead Capture

This isn't a specific strategy. It's more general advice. Focus on lead capture.

By lead capture, I mean getting people to subscribe by entering their email address on your website. Then you have a direct line of communication with them. Being able to communicate with anyone that has shared enough interest in what you do to actually hand over their email address—on your terms—is more important than words can express.

Forget about web traffic or pageviews or any of that junk. Optimize your site the best you can for capturing email addresses. Your traffic might suffer a bit, but a properly-designed internet business will be able to make at least a few dollars per subscriber, per year on average, and maybe much more. Again, it's about quality, not quantity, and having 1,000 engaged email subscribers will probably make you more money than a thousand random web hits daily—depending on how you have things set up.

Unless, of course, you have nothing to sell. But trust me, if you make a few bucks online and gather some kind of following, you'll find things to sell to them—your products or those of other people as an affiliate.

I recommend creating a basic lead capture page and trying to drive people there. A nice picture, a free offering that compels at least 10% of the people that visit that page to subscribe, and a little subscribe button is about all you need. Here's something I created for Buck Books, for example:

Haven't tested it out yet, but I'm sure it will work just fine based on past experience with creating pages like this.

And along the same lines as other advice and philosophizing that I've done prior: Be genuine, cool, awesome, unsalesy, and so forth with these people once they subscribe. Build trust. Give them great value and don't charge them anything for it. At least not at first. Demonstrate, in the words of famous internet business icon Frank Kern, "shock and awe coolness."

You want these people to love you for life and still be eagerly opening your emails years from now. To do that, you can't dive right in to selling them some shit. And you certainly can't promise them a "free eBook" that turns out to be four pages long that touts the miraculous benefits of some outrageously expensive product you just-so-happen to sell on your website. Lemme guess, it's marked down to some absurdly low price if you buy within the next hour!

That may be an effective way to convert a first-time visitor into a customer quickly, but that's not how you are going to build an army of email subscribers that will buy a bag of rocks gathered by you years down the road (I know one guy with a strong cult following on the internet that actually charges people $500 to hang out with him for a day stacking rocks. Not even joking. Seriously man, these people paid $500 to stack rocks).

Philosophies on this kind of thing vary tremendously, but again, my prediction is that the current trend of increasing distaste for stuff that has the feel of being an advertisement will soon become complete intolerance. I strongly believe that advertising will one day lose its effectiveness. It's already underway. My 9-year old daughter already yells "fucking commercials!" at her laptop every time one starts playing. That's my girl.

Anyway, long story short, rock-stacking tangents aside, nearly all internet businesses should make gathering quality email subscribers the top priority. Knowing this from the get go will certainly expedite the time it takes you to reach a satisfying level of success.

Host Events

Now we're really getting somewhere! While online events of various shapes and flavors are becoming a little worn out and watered down, a well-done event is still, by far, the best way to reach success online in a short period of time. One of my online amigos and colleagues has run two events this year and managed to draw in more than 150,000 email subscribers and countless backlinks to his website (which helps your site perform better in search engines, for those that don't know that). Now, with over 150,000 email subscribers, there's really no way to screw that up. That's some lifetime financial security right there.

My baby, Buck Books, was heavily inspired by a popular type of event online known as a "book bundle." In fact, the first person to ever construct a book bundle as far as I know, Todd Dosenberry, now works for Buck Books. He was praying and hoping to sell 500 units of his first bundle at $39, and ended up bringing in around $300,000 in revenue in five days. That got my attention!

The playbook for book bundles is to get a bunch of authors with a decent online following together, throw all of their books into one bundle (the masters at Ultimate

Bundles just did one with over 70 books for something like $29), and then get all of the authors plus some outside affiliates to promote the event, which is limited to a few days or so. Affiliates and authors alike get a nice share of the sale price when someone purchases that rode in on their link—usually 50-75%, and the host keeps a little dough and a nice, juicy list of subscribers.

Basically, you are creating a great way for people with a following online to make some money, and they do so by driving a bunch of traffic over to your site. Mutually beneficial I tellz ya. That's exactly how I built Buck Books. It made over $1,000 on its first day. The gang over at Ultimate Bundles just did an event to the tune of $700,000 of revenue or so. Their server collapsed at one point during the event the traffic was so heavy.

Boy that sure beats writing a zillion blog posts and waiting for Google to give you props in their algorithm.

Another popular type of event that has blown up in the last few years to the point of absurdity is the "online summit." Again, I know many who have snatched up as many as 100,000 email subscribers or more in a matter of days. After getting all of these email subscribers, they went on to promote various affiliate offers in their niche, typically making five figures per email broadcast.

With an online summit, the typical playbook is to interview as many people in a particular niche that have a decent following as possible, provide access to the interviews when they come out for one day only, then package all of the interviews into one product available for sale. Participants in the summit will promote their talk to their own followers using an affiliate link, and if any of those people end up purchasing the entire collection of interviews, the participant will get a cut. Outside affiliates love to promote these events, too. Many bloggers make a substantial portion of their annual revenue from promoting book bundles and summits in their niche.

Don't start out on YouTube and wait for the world to find you. Don't type your little fingers to the bone waiting for Google to start putting you at the top of the search engine rankings. Unless you have visible abs or gigantic breasts, doing that might take you a half decade just to get to the point where you're making $1,000 per month. Try this shortcut out. It also happens to be a great way, perhaps the best way, to network with big influencers that have thousands of perfect candidates to become your customers.

But be warned. These events are getting stale in a hurry because every little dick player on earth is trying to put one together. Either think of a new twist (like I did with the creation of one of my websites, www.180radio.com, or like Kevin Gianni did when he decided to host heated recorded debates between arch rivals in the health and nutrition community), or, if you plan to follow these basic templates, go all out. By all out, I mean *all out*. The landing page must be perfect. The interviews must be awesome. You must get everyone involved to actually sign some kind of informal agreement that they will promote the event to their email subscribers and on social media and beyond. You must have an affiliate program with a very high commission rate. You must spend months contacting every single person you can find on the internet to promote your event.

If you don't do it right the first go around, you probably won't get a second chance. Moreover, if you botch it, or it's sloppy, every single one of the influencers in your niche will forever think of you as a time-wasting tool. But if you do get it right, you could be making five figures monthly just a few months into your internet business career. The internet entrepreneurs that have had the quickest rise to success that I have communicated with personally have all gotten there with events.

Go On a Blog Tour

It's some work. And it ain't easy to just get a gig on someone's site as a guest blogger. But going on a blog tour—as in reaching out to hundreds of bloggers and websites in an attempt to write an article on that site—is a much faster way to garner a lucrative following online than simply blogging your ass off on your own site for your mom and sister to read.

I bet at least 500 people have written to me over the years asking if they could write a blog post on a website of mine. But it was always some scammy crap. However, when someone wrote to me and sounded like a human being, I was totally open and receptive to the idea. Make sure your email requests to write an article or guest blog post are written with personality and flavor, and that they mention something very specific about the person's work that shows them you're not just another scammer.

Here's a perfect example of what your email should NOT sound like. I copied and pasted it verbatim with "English Clearly Ain't My First Language" mistakes intact and that totally fictitious name, "Ruby Andrew." I literally got this the same day I wrote this chapter:

Hello!

Hope you are doing well!

I visited your blog "http://180degreehealth.com/" earlier today and just wanted to congratulate you on a well presented, and informative blog. I have an article which has content relevant to your site. I am interested to do guest post submission.

As per google update we all know that unique and relevant content is more important for a blog. So I want to submit related article or post on your site, and I just need one clean back link in return either in the authorbio/in the body of the article. So if you are interested please inform me soon.

And here is my Google+ link to check my published articles in different blogs.

https://plus.google.com/u/0/103033005097013090219/posts

Awaiting for your reply,

Thanking you,

With Kind Regards,

Ruby Andrew.

Wow. That was painful. Glad that's over.

What's also cool about blog touring is that your own website can be set up to gather leads, perhaps putting them through some kind of interesting eCourse to help familiarize them with you and build trust before you ever dare to try to sell them something. Put another way, you can send people back to a lead page from each of these guest blog posts and articles, and make more efficient use of those clicks to your site than if they had come to read an article of yours on your very own site.

Okay, that was still a horrible explanation. Let me put it to you like this:

When I wrote articles on my blog and had little "Hey, enter your email to get some bodaciously awesome free stuff" signup forms all over the blog, I got a 0.2% conversion rate, or about ten new subscribers per 5,000 visits. When I send traffic to a simple lead page that has only two options—enter your email address or leave—I usually get a 10-20% conversion rate, or 500-1,000 email subscribers per 5,000 visits. Big difference.

For more on blog touring, try reading my buddy Tom's book: *Guest Blogging Goldmine*. I haven't read the book, but I know the author well. He definitely gets it. So I'm sure it's got some good stuff in there.

Go On a Podcast Tour

Ditto the blog tour, but with podcasts. Go invite yourself onto a bunch of podcasts and appear before audiences that took years for the host to build. It's a great shortcut, but I don't find it to be quite as effective as going on a blog tour. Articles get read a lot more than podcasts get listened to. But if you're a good speaker and a terrible writer, it could be a better alternative. It's often a lot more time efficient as well, unless you write stupidly fast like King Buck does.

There are other types of tours you could do as well. For example, if you are wanting to blow up your YouTube channel and make money off of your success there, the same general strategy applies. Go out and try to get some of your videos posted on other channels. Invite other YouTubers to do a video-recorded debate. Network with others that have already got that audience built to the best of your ability, and find some way to reciprocate. It can be slow going at first if you only have 20 subscribers to your channel, but you'll still reach success a lot faster by branching out and networking with others from the beginning instead of being your own one person island waiting for the world to just happen to stumble across your work.

Start a Podcast

Better than going on a podcast tour is to actually start your own podcast. Sitting down and speaking with someone for an hour or so in a recorded interview is very intimate. I've been on at least 20 podcasts over the years, and I remember the host that interviewed me very well—typically having conversations with them about all kinds of things months and even years after we first "met" for a recorded talk.

While some big influencers may get enough interview requests that they start to decline invites if it appears that the audience they'll be heard by is too small, most will be grateful for any opportunity to put their voice in the ears of new people. I have turned down only a handful of interviews over the years, and as many times as I've seen huge icons appear on relatively small podcast shows, I'm pretty sure that even a podcasting newbie will have some immediate success in landing interviews with some pretty significant guests.

When someone appears on your podcast, they will often let people know when the interview comes out—at the very least on social media—just as a common courtesy to the person doing the interviewing. This can be a great direct jumpstart to your success online, aside from the importance of having dozens of influencers know who you are and remember your name.

You can also put your podcast recordings, with or without video, on YouTube for extra exposure beyond what you'll get from having your podcast over on iTunes or Blogtalk Radio, or wherever you decide to focus on.

All in all, podcasting works, it's as good of a networking tool as just about anything, and it's relatively easy to do. Each podcast will require just three to four hours of your time to get posted. If you're a talker and love having conversations with interesting people, this won't feel the least bit like work. It will be effortless, and when each episode requires just a few hours of your time, you can be posting new podcasts almost constantly in your first few months to get on your "web feet" quickly.

Create an Affiliate Program

Creating an affiliate program, if you have little to no technical computer experience, can sound daunting. However, it's usually quite easy to set up, doesn't cost that much, and, with a little practice, is pretty easy to operate and figure out. I recommend, no matter what you sell, that you implement some kind of affiliate program for it immediately. Don't wait.

Affiliate programs are awesome for several reasons. The first is that you only have to pay someone when they actually sell something, or, in the case of Buck Books, when someone actually becomes a subscriber.

Over the years I've tried advertising on Google Adwords. I poured thousands into search engine optimization. I poured thousands more into backlinking. I poured more thousands into Facebook advertising. The problem is that I put a bunch of money into those things, but whether it led to more sales or not, the price was still the same. And I've yet to pour a bunch of money into something that got a positive return on investment.

With an affiliate program, however, you really can't lose money. If an affiliate of yours drives a bunch of traffic over to your site and they buy nothing, you don't lose a nickel.

You might have a bummed out affiliate that won't promote your stuff ever again, but at least you didn't have to drop kwan to find out that your site doesn't convert very well.

Never drop kwan!

Once again, I will remind you that trust is the top commodity on the internet, and that's yet another reason why affiliate programs will typically outperform any kind of dry advertising you could ever think of doing.

With advertisements, the person clicking on an ad will immediately have distrust. Most people have subscribed to enough scammy email lists and bought enough mediocre crap, that they just don't trust something that they don't know anymore. However, an affiliate will typically be a real person with a list of people that they've built great trust and rapport with. An endorsement from a person like this is extremely valuable. Let me tell you a little story to help you understand just how powerful an endorsement from a trusted authority can be...

Once upon a time I was blogging my little heart out. At the time, despite getting tens of thousands of visits to my website every month, I was only making about $1,000 a month from sales of my eBooks. It was tough for me to really envision making much more than that. I had made up to $2,000 per month for a very short while, but it had faded. Without releasing a new book or something along those lines, it just didn't seem like there was much action going on despite getting hundreds of new comments on my blog each week and having great engagement with the people that did follow my work.

Then I took a little trip to the wondrous state of West Virginia where the toothbrush was invented (if it was invented anywhere else, it would have been called a "teethbrush"). There I shadowed an alternative health practitioner doing some really unique stuff that I had taken an interest in. I started writing about this guy, humbled by some of the new things I was learning from him, and humbled further still by talking to many of the clients that had come into his office having overcome stage four breast cancer and other seemingly incurable ailments.

This guy was making money in three ways primarily: he offered consultations by phone, he sold testing kits to monitor your body chemistry at home, and he sold supplements that were dosed out based on the results of the home tests.

With me writing about how promising this type of nutritional therapy appeared to be in a lengthy series of blog posts, this guy went from almost closing his doors to having his phone ringing off the hook. People drove from hours away to visit with him in person. Others considered flying in with their whole families to stay at a nearby hotel (more like a roach-infested crackhouse), and people all over the world began consulting with him, ordering test kits, and ordering supplements.

Based on the price of his offerings, and the sheer volume of test kits I saw getting put into boxes and dropped off at the post office (I carried many of them over there myself), I figure he brought in between $40,000-60,000 in revenue the first month I was there. No joke.

Here I was saying "Hey, buy my books!" to a trusted audience and making a measly $1,000 per month, and then I tell the same people that this guy really might have some answers that could help them, and those same people were dropping $600 like it was hot. It was crazy. And I learned a powerful lesson, and that is:

Recommending someone else's products and services leads to more sales than trying to sell your own stuff.

By the same token, the results you'll get from a strong recommendation from someone else will be far better than anything you will ever do or try. And that's why affiliate programs rule. I'd go so far as to say that people on the internet with no products or services to sell might very well make more money than those who do, because everything they sell is based on a recommendation, and most affiliate programs pay more than 50% to the affiliate. Keep that in mind as well as you start your online ventures. There's never a shortage of stuff to sell on the internet. You just have to build a following of loyal, interested leads that trust you and you're golden.

Affiliate programs are also great to have as you go about networking with the influencers in your niche. You probably don't want to email people up out of the blue and try to get them to be an affiliate for a product or service and a person they don't know. They will meet that with distrust just as we all do whenever we see something for sale on the internet (or anywhere, really). But once you get to know them and establish a little connection with them—and build a little trust—it's awfully nice to be able to ask for help and be able to offer them some money for their efforts. It's a wonderful, mutually-beneficial thing.

But don't think that just because you've created an affiliate program that anyone and everyone will be wild about promoting your product or service because there is money involved. No way Jose. Like I said, there is no shortage of things to sell on the internet, and almost everyone you encounter is very selective about what they promote—mostly because they can be. The glut of things that one can promote as an affiliate are vast enough that any savvy internet entrepreneur wouldn't dare sacrifice the trust they've built with their audience by recommending something to them that is crap. That's why you have to build trust with a potential affiliate first, show that you are all about quality and integrity first, and then, and only then, will they consider being an active affiliate for you.

If you sell anything of any kind on the internet, make sure you start an affiliate program right away and pour your heart and soul into it. There's no better way to jumpstart your success online with the exception of events, but successful events require having an affiliate program to begin with, so the two are really inseparable.

Lastly, if you're wanting to build some great online relationships, you should also consider being an affiliate for people you're wanting to build a strong connection with, and go get after it. Being an active affiliate for someone in your niche is another great gateway to getting to know that person and form a mutually beneficial relationship with them. They are much more likely to help out an affiliate of theirs than they will be to help out someone who isn't an affiliate of theirs.

Hire Freelancers

The endless array of cheap freelancers specializing in all kinds of valuable skills is changing the face of internet business. I love it. On our team we now have over 20 freelancers that live all over the world helping us do a variety of things. If things go as planned, that number will continue to grow as we grow. The luxury of being able to set your own schedule, quit your job, work from anywhere, and scale your workload up and down as needed has driven freelancer wages into the basement. It's an amazing time to take a good idea, scale it quickly, and unshackle yourself from the day to day aspects of the operation—freeing up your time for more creative endeavors or more fun and recreation. Whatever floats your boat.

When starting out with a new venture, I would strongly advise against going overboard with freelancers. Get the business up and running and making a profit. Make some mistakes yourself and correct them. Fine tune the beast into a well-oiled machine...Then bring freelancers in, directing them to do very precise things that you know are worth more money to your business than you will be paying them to do it.

If you get too carried away too early, I fear that you'll spend big dollars and be more or less unable to direct your freelancers in a way that will result in a profit—short-term or long-term. At least that's been my experience. Know how much a blog post is worth before you pay someone to write one. Know how valuable a like on Facebook is before you pay someone to build up your social networks. Or, at the very least, hire someone to do the easy stuff so you can spend more time focusing on the activities that you've identified as being the most lucrative uses of your time.

For example, I brought in people long ago to edit, proofread, and narrate our books. I use this extra time to write more books of my own and bring more subscribers into Buck Books. These people work for $25 an hour or less, and I make $100 per hour and up writing and running my other businesses with all of those hours freed up.

Anywho, hiring freelancers is not a first step to get your internet enterprise up and running. However, I do think that once you've proven your model to be successful, a large portion of the first profits that you see coming in should immediately be allocated to expansion using mostly the help of freelancers. They can run the day to day while you work on the high-priority stuff that is going to actually make a difference for your business. This isn't a first step shortcut, but it is a powerful second step shortcut that can take your internet business from small and profitable to something that can really deliver what one of my online amigos calls "end game" money. Talking six figures per month or perhaps getting bought out for eight figures— something I've definitely got in the back of my mind.

This book was launched as part of a promotion with Chris Ducker's amazing book, *Virtual Freedom*. Been too busy to read that myself, but the title and the reviews of it speak for itself. I'm sure if the topic of hiring freelancers and an army of virtual assistants excites you, this book seems like THE resource on the subject. Hopefully you had a chance to pick that one up along with this one at 99 cents.

Conclusion

Is it really over already? Dang these Buck Flogging books fly by in a hurry. Don't blink or you'll miss 'em! Hey, even I know that size doesn't matter when it comes to books. I for one believe that in today's fast-paced world with incredibly efficient information delivery, that average book length will continue to get smaller and smaller— particularly in the nonfiction realm. But really, "smaller" isn't the right word. Books are just becoming increasingly concise and tackling smaller subjects. It's a good thing. And it allows me to keep all my shiz a Buck. Buck-4-Ever!

A buck is quite a steal for the value you got in this book. The only way you might fail to earn an extra dollar or more from the information in this book is if you decide not to use it! If you do, you'll quickly find that even just reaching out and making contact with one influencer in your niche with my encouragement will bring in hundreds of dollars or more. Perhaps, like I have done with Archangel Ink, you could build an entire business from scratch to a few thousand bones per month around just a couple of communiques with the right gangstaz.

Okay, maybe "communiques" wasn't the perfect word, but it sounded nice with "couple." Hey, I've gotta narrate this thing. These kinds of things are important.

So in conclusion, I just have one final thing to share:

[Insert hilarious and inspirational paragraph]

Please, dry your tears. That's just hope and gratitude you're experiencing, just like the Rabbi at the bar hahahahaha.

Wow. Weirdest ending to a book ever.

Review this Badboy

In order to keep being able to spread the gospel of Buck Flogging for a mere buck, I really need to get an obscene amount of reviews. Would you please take just a moment to help me out? Just leave a little review on Amazon, but leave out the parts about how crass and sexist I am and how desperately I need an editor. That doesn't help so much. Use words like "genius," "hilarious," and "epic."

Thanks for your help.

I hope that the information in this book helps you out as well. I really do. That's why I wrote it. Living a no-job life is really fun. Ever since the day I achieved it I just wanted to help others do the same. From your vantage point it may seem really daunting and difficult—an impossible dream. It's not really. Nothing to it but to do it. I wish you well.

About the Author

"Giving you the Buck-naked truth about online entrepreneurship."

Hi I'm Buck Flogging. Hell yeah that's my real name and that's totally me in the picture living large and driving the ladies wild. It's definitely not just some picture from Shutterstock.

When I'm not busy squatting 800 pounds for reps and pleasing all those ladies, I'm writing lots of books, narrating audiobooks, helping authors publish and successfully sell their work, and operating some lucrative online businesses of mine.

I originally started as a know-nothing wannabe writer that was encouraged to start this mysterious thing called a "blog." From moronic mistakes and prolonged poverty I emerged seven years later with the success that all online entrepreneurs dream of achieving.

I hope to find time to write several short books revealing as much of what I've learned as possible. I love seeing other people succeed, and I hate to see others make the same mistakes I did. For more author resources, go to www.archangelink.com. For questions or comments, send those to buck@archangelink.com

Other books by Buck:

Kill Your Blog: 12 Reasons why you Should Stop $%#ing Blogging!

How to Create an Audiobook for Audible

Reviewperstar: 12 Tasteful Ways to Get More Book Reviews